I Am Enough

A Coloring Book of Reminders

Elizabeth Crooks, B.Msc.

I am Enough: A Coloring Book of Reminders

Copyright © 2016 CreateSpace Independent Publishing Platform
All Rights Reserved

ISBN: 1537597841
ISBN 13: 978-1537597843

Cover Art by Elizabeth Crooks
Interior Art by Elizabeth Crooks

For more information please visit:
www.lnlawakening.com

For those who forgot that they have always been enough:
Remember that you *always will be* enough.

INTRODUCTION

Words have power. Words form our perceptions and create our realities. When you change the words you use, your life changes as well. Words are important, and when used purposefully, they convey messages to instill constructive mindsets. Now is the time to move beyond believing that you are not worthy enough, not loveable enough, not beautiful enough and not intelligent enough. You are more than enough. We all are.

It takes 10 to 30 days to wire in a new habit. If you don't already believe that you are enough in all aspects of your life, start with these simple phrases and repeat them every day for at least 10 days, and ideally for 30 days. You have 10 days. You have 30 days. Commit to changing your own thoughts by simply reminding yourself that you are enough.

The human mind believes what it sees, what it hears, and what it experiences most often. Make feeling more than enough familiar by training yourself to believe it. Post your colored reminders around your home. Surround yourself with positive images and positive words and remind yourself each and every day, at least three times a day, until you no longer need a reminder.

Use this coloring book as just another tool on your journey of self-discovery. Use these affirmations of being enough to elevate your self-worth until you know, wholeheartedly, that you are more than enough in everything that you do and everything that you are. Choose to color and post the reminders that you resonate with, or are drawn to, first. Often these are the ones we need the most in our lives right now.

We are all more than enough in all aspects of our lives, and when we start to remember this our lives improve on many levels. Change the words you use to describe yourself for the better. Use coloring to your advantage by committing to forming a new, uplifting habit while having fun, getting creative, and relaxing to your one of your favorite pastimes

How to Use this Coloring Book

1. Color a page
2. Cut out/Tear out the page
3. Post the colored page where you will see it every day
4. Repeat the phrase in your head (three times a day*)
5. Repeat the phrase out loud (three times a day*)
6. Continue for 10-30 days until it is no longer a chore to remember that you are enough

*Three times a day ideally means three different times a day (morning, noon, and night). You can repeat the phrases in your head and out loud more than three times a day, but it helps to have a set time in the beginning to make sure you are doing the exercise throughout a given day. I set alarms on my phone to remind myself that "I am enough" while I was doing this exercise for a month. Find what works for you, but if you post the reminder where you will see it often, then it will naturally remind you throughout the day.

So, why does "I am enough" work? How does this affect me? And why should I commit to telling myself that I am enough?

Once you buy into not being enough as a child, you can believe that your entire life. Not believing that you are enough is often behind every issue we have as human beings. You came into this world as enough. You came into this world as a perfect baby who is meant to be here.

"I am enough" is a powerful phrase for its simplicity. It is so simple that the mind cannot reject it as anything but true. Logically it is true. There is no objection to "I am enough," whereas saying "I am a Goddess" or "I am a rock star" is a lot harder for the mind to believe if you have never thought you were good enough before.

"I am enough" is a simple affirmation that contradicts almost every issue known to the human mind. Many people don't feel as if they are enough, whether that is smart enough, loveable enough, worthy enough, deserving enough, beautiful enough, able enough and so on. This simple statement reverses all thoughts and beliefs of not being enough, once you believe it that is. And it takes time to believe something new. It takes practice. It isn't easy, and it doesn't have to be hard, but it is simple. Just keep at it and re-train your own brain to believe that you are enough by seeing it, hearing it, and practicing it every day until you know it to be true.

Changing one belief about yourself: that you are enough and always have been and always will be enough, will change your life. When you achieve something, say "I deserve this, because I am enough." When someone tells you they love you, say "I deserve this love, because I am enough." When someone tells you they like your hair or your outfit, say "I deserve compliments, because I am enough." You are more than enough in all aspects of your life. It is up to you to start believing it. Put in the work, for a relatively short amount of time, and just give it a try. If it doesn't change your life in a month, then no harm done; you can go back to how things were before.

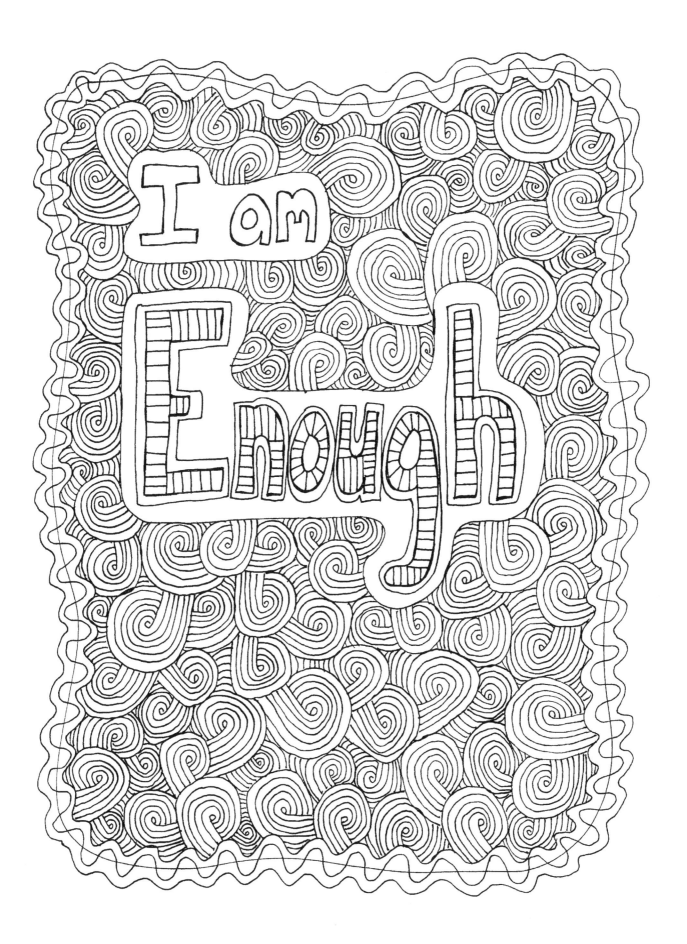

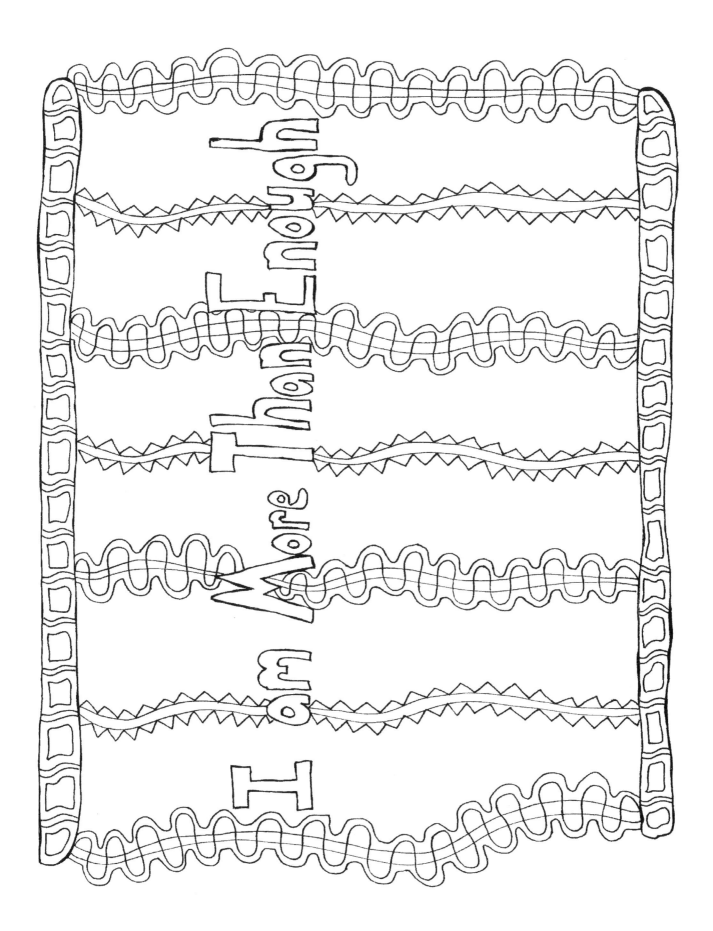

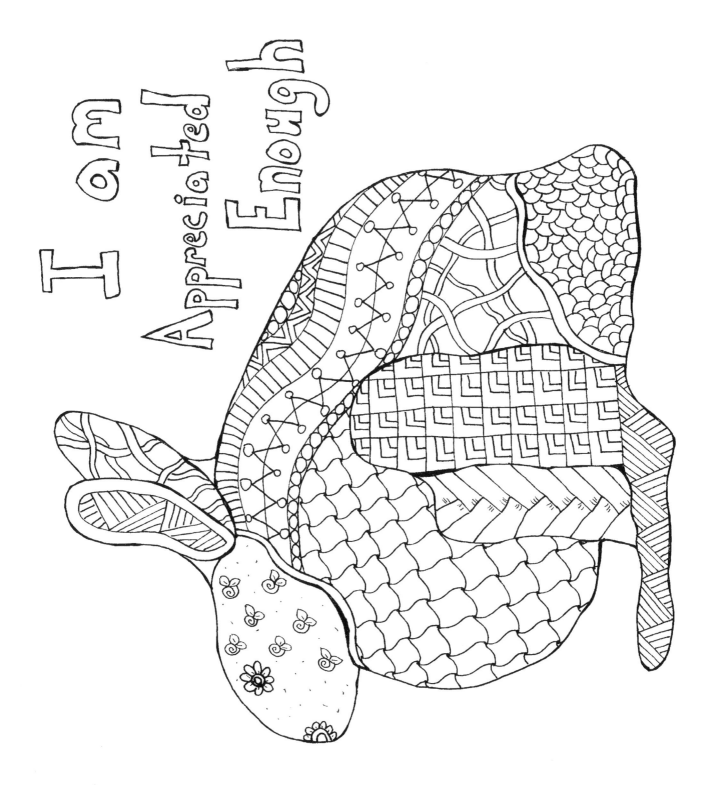

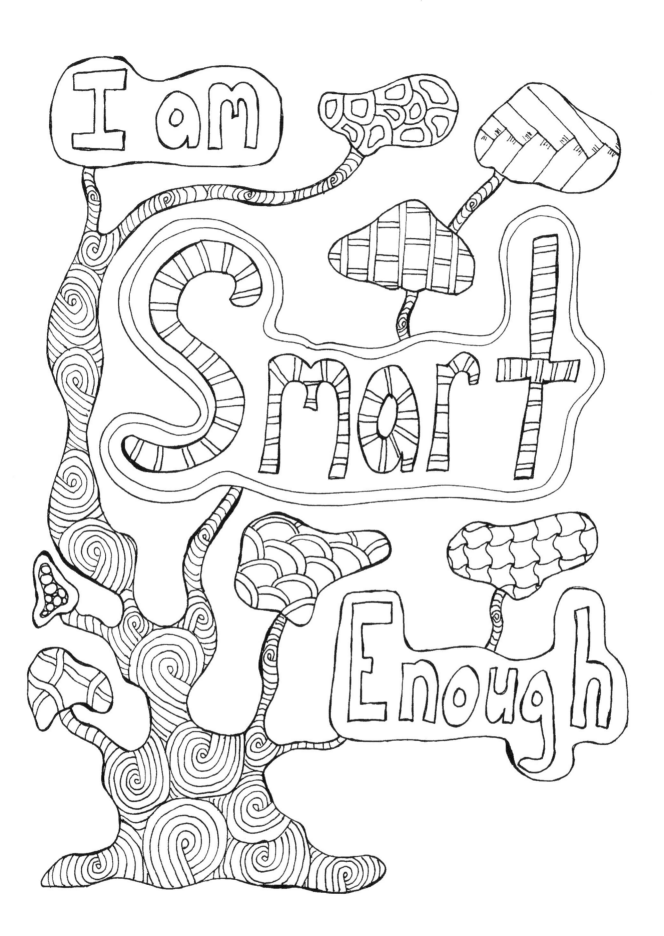

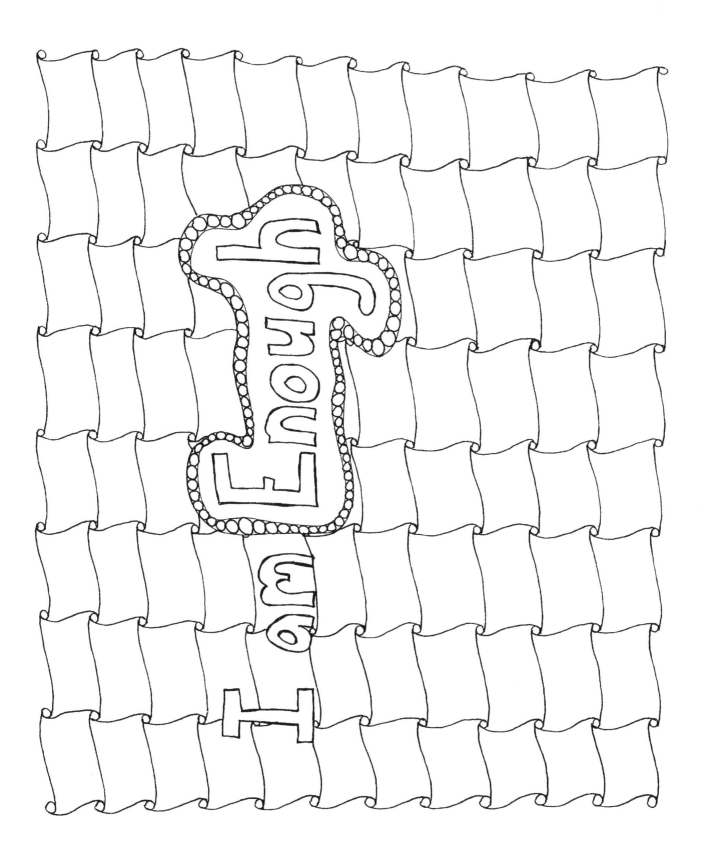

FINAL THOUGHTS

Although believing "I am enough" can assist our self-esteem and self-worth in our daily lives, I encourage everyone to create their own reminders that resonate with them and their personal journeys.

Maybe you don't believe that you are deserving or valued enough. Maybe you don't believe that you are creative or expressive enough. You are. It's just that we just have to remind ourselves that we are. The world and other people around us have given us many reasons to believe otherwise, and it is our responsibility to no longer believe that we are not enough.

Find the words that work for you and put in the effort to change the thoughts you have about yourself and your life. It can be as simple as coloring and posting a word on your bedroom wall so you will see it every day. But you also have to tell yourself that word or phrase often, and you have to want to believe it.

You can change how you see yourself, and this change can be this simple if you allow it to be. Change is only hard if you think it is. Commit to changing your own beliefs and habits by simply reminding yourself every day. This is your life. You have 10 days. You have 30 days. It is your choice to start thinking you are more than enough right now.

I wish you well on your journey of self-discovery and self-improvement. Go with the flow and trust in yourself as you commit to changing what you believe about yourself for the better.

Learn
Grow
Learn some more
And continue to Grow

Extra examples to try on your own:

Find what works for you, as this is your journey. What else do you want to be more than enough?
I am _____ Enough…

Handsome	Worthy	Valued	Likeable
Deserving	Blessed	Optimistic	Creative
Aware	Enlightened	Able	Gorgeous
Funny	Organized	Expressive	Young

Thank you for choosing this coloring book.
And thank you for choosing to make a positive, constructive change in your life.
When we all make changes for the better, the world changes for the better as well.

ABOUT THE AUTHOR

Elizabeth Crooks is a writer, author, artist and guide who shares her knowledge of consciousness, awareness, and the human experience, emphasizing the art of mindfulness and living from the heart. She holds a Bachelors of Metaphysical Sciences degree (B.Msc.) from the University of Metaphysical Sciences, and is a certified Reiki Master with years of energy work experience. When she is not sharing her knowledge through writings and art, she spends her time reading, traveling, walking in nature, and doodling in love. She is a published author on books pertaining to metaphysical sciences and personal growth, as well as several conscious coloring books for both adults and children.

For more information, please visit www.lnlawakening.com

And if you like the cover design, turn the page and color it in.
Thank you!

Made in the USA
Middletown, DE
30 April 2018